1001 Batty Books

A Collision of Book Titles and Awful Authors

Derek Good & Craig McFadyen

ISBN-13:978-1517630430

ISBN-10:1517630436

DEDICATION

This book is dedicated to all those people whose names are so aptly linked to their job titles that together they sound unbelievably funny. You have provided us with many moments of classic fun. Thanks for giving us a reason to write this book and for giving us something to laugh about!

CONTENTS

A BRIEF HISTORY OF BATTY BOOKS

Through the mists of time, we have retraced the steps of the pioneers of each civilization to have pondered the irony of book title coupled with its author. As far back as the Egyptian empire, a scholar by the name of *Mesi Ryter* stored handwritten scrolls in the Great Library. For many years these writings were thought to be hieroglyphics but turned out to be Mesi's own compilation of 'Batty Biblio' that few could read. Thanks to the famous Middle Eastern gossip columnist, *Mustapha Secret*, news of the Batty Books became widespread. A Greek philosopher called *Hissy Fittus* compiled an anthology of Batty Books works in Athens but threw a tantrum when his compilation was ridiculed in court. His works were lost for many years.

A mad Captain in the Persian army by the crazy but aptly named *Hussein Anywae* was so impressed with the Great Library he encountered in Alexandria that he went on search for the 'Batticus Bookitus' and as legend has it he stole the works of the Greeks only to lose them to the Romans. Never to miss out on something big, the Roman Emperor *Caeser Nopportunitie* grabbed the compiled works of 'Pugno Libro' and took them to the safety of the great Latin city. However, the works were lost after the fall of Rome.

Occasionally the world would hear of someone somewhere who claimed to have discovered fragments of the Batty Books original compilation. A member of The Korean royal family called *Prince Lee Sum* paid a fortune for a handful of pages thought to be recovered from the ruins of Ancient Rome. The history books showed even the Aztecs somehow claimed them when one of their explorers, *Itchi Feet* had travelled to the mythical old world in a canoe.

It wasn't until the Renaissance that any viable claim could be verified. The French Magician, *Cardinal Hisleeves* seemingly out of nowhere presented Louis XV with a short volume of Batty Books – 'Le Livres de

Batty' at his coronation. These were on display for many years thanks to the promoter *X. E. Bichon*. The same collection ended up in England when the last noble monk *Benny Diction* rescued them from the continent and stored them under what is now an ice cream factory. In the 1970s, one of the workers, *Isla Vasinglecone* found the old papers and presented the idea as a gimmick for ice lolly sticks. They were a minor success and schoolboys around the country enjoyed sharing the Batty Books in school playgrounds.

This current work realises part of the schoolboy memories and fond appreciation for irony that seldom can rival that of a Batty Book or an Awful Author. Enjoy!!!!

ACCIDENTS

1. In a Car Accident by Rhea Ender

2. Who Put That There? by Ai Bang Mai Nee

3. Man on Ice by Betty Slips

4. Run Over by Moe Down

5. Finding Floor Traps by Isadore There

6. Covering all Bases by Justin Case

7. Unsafe Driving by Lewis Wheel

8. What Went Wrong by Mal Funkshun

9. A Close Call by Marge Innall

10. Slow Accident Recovery by Estelle Hertz

ACTING & MOVIES

11. I'm in the Movies by Holly Wood

12. Stunt Man by Iris Klife

13. Recording Actors by Phil Murr

14. Making Movies by Dai Rector

15. Lewis Carrol by Alison Wonderland

16. Gold at the End of the Rainbow by L. Dorado

17. French Movie Censorship by Yvette Ze Movie

18. Microphone Testing by Juan Tu Threigh

19. Testing Audio Sound by Mike Czech

20. Just a Stuntman by Willie Die

ANGER MANAGEMENT

21.That's not Happening by Noah Way

22. It Could be Hell by Val Halla

23. Riled up the Wrong Way by Anne Tagonise

24. Rude Awakening by I. Ripacoverov

25. NO! by Kurt Replie

26. Don't Touch Me by Leigh Voff

27. Not my Friend by N. Emmie

28. Insults Start Here by U. Pigg

29. Getting Worked Up by Anne Noyyed

30. Getting Angry by A. Gressive

ANIMALS

31. German Sheep Dog by Al Sation

32. Large Reptiles by Ali Gator

33. A Mongoose by Amir Katt

34. Flat Fish by Hal E. Butt

35. Examine Animals by Dai Seckshun

36. Hard Working Horses by Clyde Dales

37. Very Small Fish by Anne Chovy

38. Aardvarks and their Habits by Ant Eaters

39. Texan Anteaters by R. Madillo

40. Large Snakes by Anna Conda

ANIMALS 2

41. Fleas and Other Pests by Ivan Itch

42. Where are the Farm Animals? by Daryn Debarn

43. Being an Ass by Don Key

44. All about Horses by E. Quine

45. Large African Mammals by Ellie Fant

46. Bull Fighting by Matt Adore

47. Letting Animals Loose by Freda Lyons

48. The Animals are Out by Gay Topen

49. Longest Neck in the Jungle by Gee Raffe

50. Annoying Insects by Amos Keeto

ANIMALS 3

51. More Annoying Insects by Anne Uthamosquito

52. Love of Elephant Tusks by Ivor Ree

53. Pet Monkeys by Jim Pan Zee

54. Blood Sucking Bugs by Lee Chez

55. Where Frogs Live by Lily Pond

56. Murmuring Mice by Mona Little

57. It's a Dog's Life by Nora Bone

58. Tiger Attacks by Nora Leggov

59. Affection for Animals by Pat Midogg

60. Working at the Zoo by C. Lion

ANIMALS 4

61. Massive Fish by Rod Broken

62. Lizards and Newts by Sal Amanda

63. Piles of Wool by Shaun Sheep

64. Hit by Cows by Stan Peed

65. No Home for The Rabbits by Warren Filled

66. Growing Up in Ponds by Tad Pohl

67. Flying Dinosaurs by Terry Dactyl

68. Reasons for Visiting a Farm by Tobias A. Pigg

69. Amphibians by Sally Mander

70. Snail Racing by Eubie Quick

ART

71. Life's a Play by Thea Terr

72. Famous Cartoons by Drew Pictures

73. Colours Don't Last by Faye Daway

74. Losing Colour by Lee Ched

75. Dull Painting by Matt Finish

76. Dramatic Speech by Moe Nalog

77. Ornamental Works of Art by Phil A. Gree

78. Modernistic Paintings by R.T. Farty

79. An Artist's Workplace by Stu Deo

80. He's No Artist by Drew Lousy

CHILDREN

81. Potty Training by Anita Pu

82. Forgotten Child by Homer Lone

83. Naughty Schoolboy by Enid Λ. Spankin

84. Another Baby Coming by Maud Ipers

85. Happy Children by Merrill E. Attplay

86. Problem Kids by Miss B. Havior

87. Cuddly Toys by Ted. E. Bear

88. Are Parents Necessary? by I. Needham

89. Kids on Horses by G. G. Riding

90.Baby Sitting Support by Justin Casey Howls

CLOTHING & FASHION

91. Cover your Back by Jack Ette

92. Japanese Dress Code by Kim Ono

93. Formal Attire by Beau Tye

94. Perfectly Presented by E. Makulet

95. Find Relief by Gertcha Corsett-Orff

96. Fresh Shirts by Preston Ironed

97. Showing off Clothes by Manny Kinn

98. Sixties Fashion by Minnie Skirt

99. Going Commando by Nicholas Girls

100. Does My Bum Look in This? by Hugh Jass

COMMUNICATION

101. The Post Script by Adeline Extra

102. All the Letters by Alf A. Bett

103. Mixing Letters by Anna Gram

104. My Pseudonym by Nick Name

105. Understanding Messages by Dee Cypher

106. Recording Conversations by Dick Tafone

107. Electronic Communications by E. Maille

108. Real Names by Monic Kerr

109. Contain Correspondence by N. V. Lope

110. Speaking Coherently by Art Iculate

COMMUNICATION 2

111. No Decision Yet by Penn Ding

112. Bad Phone Connections by R. U. There

113. Native Dialects by Verne Accula

114. All the Answers by Sol Ooshan

115. Call Me by Tel E. Fone

116. Telecommunications by Kaye Bull

117. Internet Connections by Moe Demm

118. Did I get that Wrong? by Miss Taken

119. Wrong Way to Say Something by Kurt Wurds

120. Now I Understand by Ria Lies

CONSTRUCTION

121. Roof Repairs by Lee King

122. The Secret of Skyscrapers by Bill Dupp

123. Long Surviving Structures by Bill Talast

124. A Builders Guide to Pricing Jobs by Bill Wright

125. Destroyed Buildings by D. Molish

126. Dry Roofing by Dwayne Pipe

127. Ugly Public Buildings by I. Saw

128. Church Towers by Belle Free

129. Asian Walls by Lee Ning

130. Houses are Made by Bill Ding

CONSTRUCTION 2

131. Produce in Quantity by Manny Facture

132. Construction Workers by Manuel Labor

133. Irish Double Glazing by Paddy O'Doors

134. Damaging Property by Van Dhal

135. Collapsing House by Sue D. Builder

136. Makeshift Village by Shan T. Town

137. Keep Out! by Barb Dwyer

138. Famous Buildings in Paris by I. Phil Towa

139. Storage Systems for the Home by Anita Garage

140. Fixing Roads by Jack Hammer

CRIME

141. House is Secure by Al Armed

142. Warning Others by Al Armist

143. It's a Robbery by Andy Tover

144. Rampaging the Village by Barb Aryan

145. Lock it Up by C. Curity

146. Grab her Bag by Caesar belongings

147. Escaped Convicts by Caesar Chance

148. Illegally Gained Money by D. Fraud

149. Vehicle Thefts by Nick McCarr

150. Slow Escapes by Doug Witherspoon

CRIME 2

151. Who Killed Elvis? by Howard I. Know

152. Harboring Fugitives by Hu Yu Hai Ding

153. Wrecking the Streets by I. Van de Lyze

154. Keeping out Burglars by Isadore Strong

155. Crossing Roads by Jay Walker

156. Stealing Cars by Joy Rider

157. Planning Robberies by Kay Singajoint

158. Prison Break Near a Forest by Lucinda Woods

159. Caught in a Snare by N. Trapment

160. Robbery in Progress by Hans Upp

CRIME 3

161. Security Searches by Pat Medown

162. Police Chase by Paul Over

163. The Witness by Esau M. Dooitt

164. Murderous Parents by Phil E Cide

165. Charged with a Crime by Ria Cuse

166. Getting Away With It by Scott Free

167. Grievous Bodily Harm by Vi O. Lent

168. Catching Robbers by U. R. Nicked

169. In your Own Prison Cell by Saul E. Terry

170. Highway Robberies by Stan and Del Liver

DAILY STUFF

171. Smooth Legs by Che Ving

172. Lose Weight by Dai Etting

173. Hideous Scalps by Dan Druff

174. Health and Fitness by Jim Geer

175. Daily Shave by Ray Zorr

176. Being Transparent by I. C. Threwit

177. A Day on the Lake by Rhoda Boat

178. Up and Down Days by C. Saw

179. Are We Happy? by Dewey Care

180. Working Out by X. R. Size

DRIVING

181. Good Valet Service by Anita Carr

182. Only Drive Japanese by Lisa Honda

183. Dangerous Car by Lou Sweel

184. Four Stable Wheels by Mike Arr

185. Are we there Yet? by Miles Away

186. Tow Away Zones by No Pah King

187. Cleaner Automobiles by Wa Shing Ka

188. Smooth Streets by Humphrey Rhodes

189. Car Prangs by Den Ted

190. Russian Car Parking by Valet Dropov

EDUCATION

191. Play School Activities by Andrew A. Picture

192. Here's Something New by Ivan I. Deer

193. High Achiever by Bess Ting-Klass

194. Great Term at School by C. Myra Port

195. Other Meanings by Connor Tayshun

196. All the Words you Need by Dick Shenary

197. Order of Library Books by Duey Decimal

198. Calling Out Loud by Heidi Claire

199. Learning from Others by Howard Yu Duit

200. Explosion in the Science Lab by Benson Burner

EDUCATION 2

201. Showing you How it Works by I. Demo

202. Things to Write with by Pen Sill

203. School Sports by Jim Nasium

204. Online Books by Kindle Ready

205. Basic Facts by L.M. Entary

206. Bad Exam Scores by Marcus Downe

207. Top Marks by Max E. Mumm

208. Small Thinking by P. Brain

209. Riveting Books by Paige Turner

210. Top of the Class by Jean E Uss

EDUCATION 3

211. Deep Thinking by Phil O'Soffie

212. More Places to Study by Polly Tecknic

213. All the Answers by Tex T. Book

214. The Name of the Book by Ty Till

215. Places to Study by Una Versity

216. Literary Giant by Rhoda Booke

217. The Whole Thing by N. Tyrely

218. Learning the Basics by Reid Enright

219. Updating the Contents by Reeve Eyes

220. Love of Large Books by Warren Peace

EMPLOYMENT

221. Producing Electricity by Jenny Rator

222. Good Research by Anna Lyst

223. Jobs for Hunchbacks by Belle Ringa

224. Struggling for Work by Bennie Fishery

225. Personal Assistants by Carrie Mai Baggs

226. Busted Down by D. Moated

227. Trapeze Artists by Dan Glynn

228. Not Good Enough for the Job by Dee Moted

229. Get Someone Else to Do it by Del E. Gate

230. Gold Mining by Doug A. Hole

EMPLOYMENT 2

231. Previous Undertaking by Doug Graves

232. Long Hours by Ernest Worker

233. Delivering Cars by Ford Parker

234. Rest from Work by Holly Day

235. Rotten Teeth by I. Pullem

236. Shove your Job by Icke Witt

237. The Hunchback Listens by Isabel Ringing

238. Management Mistake by Ivor E. Tower

239. Tyre Mechanics by Jack Tupp

240. Change of Career by Robin Banks

EMPLOYMENT 3

241. Flooring Specialists by Lynn O'Leum

242. Top of the Pile by Mark Etleeder

243. No Need to Work by Mary A. Richman

244. Walking to Work by Misty Buss

245. Grass Cutting for a Job by Moe Lornes

246. Back in your Job Again by Ria Point

247. Chain Saw Skills by Tim Burr

248. Learning the Ropes by Trey Nee

249. Getting up to Speed by Trey Ning

250. Cemetery Worker by Phil Graves

FESTIVE & HOLIDAYS

251. Christmas Tunes by Carol Syngers

252. Time for Festivities by Chris Mouse

253. Get into Christmas by Don Gay Apparel

254. Shall I Invite Him? by Woody Kum

255. Happy Holidays by Mary Christmas

256. Enjoying a Long Break by Summer Hols

257. Going on Holiday by Felix Ited

258. Items from Holiday by Sue Veneer

259. Our Guest has Arrived by Wendy Gethere

260. Santa Claus Exists by I. Belle Eve

FINANCIAL

261. Small Aid by Len de Fyver

262. Avoid Missing Postage by Celia Envelope

263. Embezzling by D. Fraud

264. No Home or Money by Des Titute

265. Got Enough Cash? by Ernie Nuff

266. Working out the Cost by Esther Mates

267. Golden Rims by Gil Tedged

268. Loads of Money by Ivor Fortune

269. Winning the Lottery by Jack Pott

270. Losing Streak by Betty Loses

FINANCIAL 2

271. Plenty of Money by Lester Worryabout

272. Money Running Out by Bill Stoupay

273. Different Economies by Moe Knees

274. Raising the Value by N. Harnsing

275. Flat Broke by Penny Less

276. Making Millions by Rich Feller

277. Money is Short by Titus Canbee

278. Living Well by Ty Coon

279. In Need of Cash by Robin da Bank

280. Filthy Rich by Millie O' Nare

FLIGHT

281. Tropical Birds by Ivor Toocan

282. Long Distance Travel by Father Roff

283. Moving Overseas by Emma Grate

284. Flying People Around by Ionna Plain

285. Turbulent Air Travel by Ivana Herl

286. Ready for Take-off by Lorne Schpad

287. Stuck at the Airport by Mr. Flight

288. Airport Security by Pat Downe

289. Taking Flight by A.V. Ation

290. Sea Birds by Al Batross

FOOD & COOKING

291. Can't Stop Drinking by Al Koholik

292. Eating Outdoors by Alf Resco

293. Strong Tasting Fish by Ann Chovie

294. Strong Tasting Sweets by Anna Seed

295. Cocktail Maker by Bart Ender

296. Strong Vegetables by Artie Choke

297. Too Much Dough by Baker Lott

298. Summer Cooking by Barb E. Cue

299. No More Drinks by Bart Abfull

300. Extreme Thirst by Annie da Drink

FOOD & COOKING 2

301. Tasty Green Dips by Basil Pesto

302. Round Red Veggies by Bea Troot

303. Eating Too Fast by Betty Chokes

304. Arabic Condiments by Sultan Vinegar

305. Beef Jerky by Bill Tong

306. Opening Crayfish by Buster Crabbe

307. Make It Weak by Dai Luting

308. Quick Chinese Meals by Chris P. Noodles

309. Pork Meals by Chu Yorr Fat

310. Yummy Breakfast by Chris P. Bacon

FOOD & COOKING 3

311. Time to Eat by Dean R. Bell

312. Gourmet Food by Dee Lishus

313. Dinner's Ready by Lady Table

314. The Big Feast by Del Vin

315. Cakes and More by Della Katessen

316. Changing Colours of Fruit by Diane Apple

317. Soft Tea Snacks by Duncan Biscuits

318. Asian and Dutch Food by Dinesh Ready

319. Great Greek Food by Donna Kebab

320. Hamburger Condiments by Dill Piccle

FOOD & COOKING 4

321. Sugary Treats by Duncan Doe Nutts

322. No More Thank You by E. Nuff

323. Can you Eat This? by Eddie Bull

324. Who Stole my Baking? by Henrietta Kookie

325. Fast Food Habits by Friar Burgher

326. Highball Cocktails by Gin Anne Tonic

327. Simple Sandwiches by Hammond Cheese

328. Bits in Chocolate by Hazel Nutts

329. She Loves Vegetables by Henrietta Carrot

330. Hot Dogs for Lunch by Frank Furter

FOOD & COOKING 5

331. I'm a Vegetarian by Herb Avore

332. Gigantic Fruit by Hugh Japples

333. Taste of the South by K. John Chicken

334. Fish Prepared by Phil A. Ted

335. Nothing to Drink by M. T. Bottle

336. Sticky Breakfast Sauces by Mabel Sirrup

337. Quickly Cooked Food Recipes by Mike Rowave

338. Favourite Chicken Meals by Nora Drumstick

339. Light Snacks by P. Nutt

340. Food on Safari by Lionel Eacher

FOOD & COOKING 6

341. Quick Lunch by Phil Drole

342. More Than One Helping by Phil Dupp

343. Another Drink Please by Phil Errup

344. Thin Slices by Phil Lay

345. I'm Thirsty by Phyllis Cupupp

346. Part of a Salad by Q. Cumber

347. Nice Smells by R. Roma

348. Small Dried Fruit by Ray Zenz

349. Topping it Up by Phil Lures

350. Cooking Chicken by Rose Ting

FOOD & COOKING 7

351. Dinner Starter by Roland Butter

352. Spicy Sausage by Sal Army

353. Japanese Lunch by Sue Shee

354. Am I Really a Fruit? by Tom Arto

355. Hungry at Parties by Wes T. Grubb

356. Difficult Cooking by Sue Flay

357. Sun Dried Grapes by Ray Zin

358. Fancy Some Lunch? by Russell Upsom-Grubb

359. Waiting for Food by Sally Vating

360. The Tangy Aroma of Garlic by Francis Smellie

FUNNY

361. Just Joking by April Fools

362. Welsh Jokes by Dai Laffin

363. Exuberant Enjoyment by Gus Tow

364. You Are Hilarious by Vera Funny

365. Funny Duo by Laurel Ann Hardy

366. Silly Suggestions by Ludi Criss

367. Swedish Jokers by Per Ovclowns

368. Makes Me Laugh by Will Tikkelme

369. Famous Comedians by Yewmai Larff

370. I'll Make you Laugh by Joe Kerr

GEOGRAPHY

371. The South Pole by Aunt Artic

372. Stilt Walking in Pakistan by Balan Singh

373. Australian Natural Beauty by Barry R. Reef

374. Islands off America by Carrie B. Ann

375. On Top of Everest by Corey Diddit

376. Swimming the Channel by Francis Coming

377. Paris is Busy by Francis Crowded

378. Antarctic Ocean by I. C. Waters

379. The Tower of Piza by Lena Little

380. The Low French Wall by Pierre Ovazetop

GEOGRAPHY 2

381. Swedish Sickos by Per Verts

382. Making Igloos by S. Keemo

383. Where River Meets Sea by S. Tury

384. Lost in the Desert by Wanda Ring

385. Getting Ahead in Japan by Yu Cat Chupp

386. Seven Days in Spain by Juan Week

387. Trips Through Sahara by Rhoda Camel

388. French Delicacy by S. Cargo

389. Travel Memories by C. Mai Foto

390. Scottish Greetings by C. U. Jimmy

GETTING OLDER

391. Avoid Baldness by Aaron Head

392. Another Year Older by Abbey Birthday

393. Looking Younger by Beau Tox

394. Facelifts May be Needed by Chin Tu Fat

395. On My Last Legs by Di Ying

396. Getting Old by Jerry Atrick

397. Alcohol Effects by Sir Osis of Liver

398. Out of Pain by Yootha Nasia

399. Nothing is Going Right by Sue E. Sidle

400. Painful Joints by Arthur Ritus

HEALTH & BEAUTY

401. Natural Healing by Al O. Vera

402. All About Style by Anita Haircut

403. Getting a Nose Job by Ryan O'Plasty

404. Medical Tubes by Cath Itter

405. Removing Whiskers by Che Verr

406. Stranded in the Desert by Dee Hydration

407. No Fat Here by Finn Bloke

408. Women's Diseases by Guy Nicology

409. Reason to Visit the Doctor by Ivor Payne

410. Safety Lifting by Ben Janees

HEALTH & BEAUTY 2

411. Tiny Germs by Mai Crobes

412. Pure Sugar by Moe Lasses

413. Healthier Life by Nosmo King

414. Feeling A Little Sad by Mel N. Colly

415. Big Bosomed Women by Phil Yerbrah

416. You Need to Diet by Wai Yu Mun Ching

417. Not Embarrassed by Frieda Look

418. Feeling Great by N. Dorfins

419. Simply Great by Dee Liteful

420. Putting on Weight by O. B. City

HISTORY

421. Ancient Treasures by Art E. Facts

422. History of the Earth by Roxanne Mi-Nerals

423. Understanding My Life by June O. Watimeen

424. Lost Cities by Ova Runn

425. 1960's America by Rachel Tensions

426. Robin Hood Fed the Poor by Robin de Rich

427. Kings and Queens by Roy L. Tee

428. Old Age Punishments by Tanya Hyde

429. Galley Slaves by Rowan Hard

430. 65 Million Years Ago by Dai Nosores

HOBBIES

431. The Female Artist by Andrew Pictures

432. Taking a Picture by Cam Ra

433. Asian Disco King by Dan Singh

434. Record Collections by Al Bumm

435. Know your Ancestors by Jenny Allergie

436. Light Reading by Maggie Zeen

437. Country Dancing by May Polle

438. Collecting Stamps by Phil Atalist

439. Flicking Objects with Fingers by Phil Lipping

440. Korean Photography by Fo To Shoot

HOME & GARDEN

441. Good Around the House by Andy Mann

442. Good Maid Services by Anita Home

443. Tupperware Storage Secrets by Anita Larder

444. Manicured Gardens by Anita Lorne

445. Old Furniture by Anne Teek

446. This House is Mine by Bill Jerome Holme

447. Above your Head by C. Ling

448. Comfortable Chairs by Chester Field

449. Handy Furniture by Chester Draws

450. Hiding in Glass Houses by C. U. There

HOME & GARDEN 2

451. Necklaces of Flowers by Daisy Chain

452. Cold Draft by Dora Jarr

453. Come on in! by Doris Open

454. Correct Furniture Placements by Feng Shui

455. Whirlpool Baths by Jack Uzi

456. Household Renovations by Peyton Decorate

457. Tepid Water by Luke Warm

458. Comfortable Couches by Moe Haire

459. Leads to the Garden by Pat E.O. Dors

460. Grass Cutting by Lorne Moa

HOME & GARDEN 3

461. Internal Light Fittings by Phil A. Ment

462. Pot Plants by Polly Anthus

463. Seeing Clearly by Wynn Doe

464. Just One Bedroom by Stu Deoflat

465. Fitted Carpets by Walter Wall

466. Putting it on Again by Ria Ply

467. How to Move Furniture by Ria Range

468. Old House Issues by Rusty Pipes

469. Glass Light Fittings by Shandy Lear

470. Picking up the Leaves by Ray King

HUMAN BODY

471. Nether Regions by Jenny Talia

472. Tickly Throat by I. Koffalott

473. Punk Hairstyles by Moe Hawks

474. Sneezing by A. Choo

475. Can't Remember Much by Al Symers

476. Using Both Hands by Amber Dextrous

477. Crouching Down by Ben Ding

478. Stretch your Back by Ben Dover

479. Growing Slowly by Bud Ding

480. Great Dentistry by Anita Smile

HUMAN BODY 2

481. Refusing to Age by Dai Mahair

482. Food Down the Wrong Pipe by Chow Konet

483. Massive Hats by E. Norma Said

484. Bolt Upright by E. Wrecked

485. Bright Lights and Loud Noises by Ed Akes

486. No Energy Required by F. Ertless

487. Changing Appearances by Faye Slift

488. Falling Asleep by Drew P. Eyes

489. Black and Blue by I. Bruce Eseely

490. Broken Razor by Harry Beard

HUMAN BODY 3

491. Cold Extremities by I. C. Finger

492. Utter Relief by I. P. Freely

493. Bend Your Arms by L. Bowe

494. No Brains by M. T. Head

495. Trouble with Drinking by Norma Leigh Lucid

496. Bigger than Most by O. Beese

497. Extra Mammary Glands by Ooja Nikanippelov

498. Good Tooth Brushing by Pearl E. Whites

499. Removing Acne by Poppa Zitt

500. Dealing with Flatulence by Hugh Farted

HUMAN BODY 4

501. Miniskirts Through History by Seymour Legg

502. Open Shirt by Seymour Skin

503. Difficulty Shaving by Rusty Blades

504. Saving your Legs by Rick Shaw

505. On Your Feet by Rose Up

506. Clean Spectacles by Seymour Wytham

507. Male Genitalia by Tess Tickles

508. The Toilet is Outside by Willie Makit

509. Badly Embarrassed by Rosie Cheeks

510. Taking a Leak by Yuri Nates

KINDNESS

511. You will get There by Eve N. Tually

512. Proper Table Manners by Eaton Wright

513. We Know How You Feel by M. Pathize

514. Let's all Go by Maude De Merryer

515. The Art of Being Generous by Miso Giving

516. Helping Others Get Around by Moe Billity

517. Looking After Others by Molly Coddelling

518. Give Your Backing by N. Dorse

519. Taking Turns by Ross Terring

520. Are you Comfortable? by Sid Down

LEGAL

521. Got Off Lightly by Lee Nient

522. Misappropriation of Funds by M. Bezzel

523. Living without Laws by Anna Kist

524. Changing my Position by Ria Line

525. Stating your Case in Court by Ivor Plee

526. Honest Citizen by Laura Byder

527. Beating Crime by Laura Norder

528. I Swear it Happened by Tess T. Money

529. That's not the way it Happened by Travis Tee

530. Under Arrest by Ivan Alibi

LET'S TALK

531. Condemning Behaviour by I. D. Nounce

532. Wishing you Well by Bess Twishes

533. Who Told Me? by Dickie Bird

534. Doing Things my Way! by Frank O'Pinion

535. Expressing Yourself by Moe Dalities

536. Peace Offerings by Olive Branch

537. Pick Up Where we Left Off by Ria Choir

538. Things Parrots Say by L. O. Polly

539. Asking the Impossible by Shirley U. Jest

540. Open Door Policy by Wanda Rinn

MAGIC

541. Making Gold by Al Kammie

542. Magic Bottles by Al Laddin

543. Gone Without a Trace by Van Isht

544. Your Future by Clare Voyance

545. The Future by Crystal Ball

546. Wishes Come True by Grant Ted

547. Casting Spells by N. Chant

548. The Fortune Teller by Reid Palms

549. Suddenly Back by Ria Peered

550. See into the Future by Chris Tallball

MARRIAGE

551. Living off Support by Ali Moaney

552. Celebrating Special Events by Annie Versary

553. Runaway Marriage by E. Lope

554. Married Woman by Hans Off

555. Loving Relationships by Rodger Knightly

556. In the Dog House by Mr. Birthday

557. Madly in Love by Q. Pidd

558. Picking up in Bars by R.U. Married

559. The Perfect Match by Sue Tabble

560. Alone at the Altar by Jill Ted

MATHEMATICS

561. Nothing Digital Here by Anna Log

562. No Straight Lines by Anne Gulls

563. Evenly Balanced by E. Quall

564. Adding Up by Juan and Juan

565. Big Numbers by Milly Onn

566. The Smallest Amount by Minnie Mumm

567. Around the Circle by Sir Cumfrence

568. Round Objects by Sir Cull

569. Go Around by Sir Cumvent

570. Simple Mathematics by Adam Upp

MEDICAL

571. Kidney Treatment by Dai Alasis

572. A Mutant is Among us by Abner Mality

573. Hospital Corners by Anita Bed

574. Stomach Gases by Belle Ching

575. Upset Tummies by Di Arrear

576. Stretch and Return by E. Lastic

577. Insomniac by Earl E. Riser

578. Needing Treatment by E. Scott Injured

579. Japanese Death by Harry Curie

580. Gum Disease by Ginger Vitus

MEDICAL 2

581. No Insomniacs Here by I. Sleepwell

582. Severe Red Lumps by Ivor Boyle

583. Food Poisoning by Sal Monella

584. Relieving the Pressure by Lance Boyle

585. Sleeping Better by Matt Tress

586. Stomach Surgery by N. Trailes

587. Addictive Substance by Nico Teen

588. Antibiotic Drugs by Penny Cillin

589. Surgery is Finished by Celia Backup

590. Need New Glasses by Kent C. Straight

MILITARY

591. Crew Cuts by Sean Head

592. Uneasy Times by Marshall Law

593. Asian Assassins at Large by Hu Yu Kill

594. Harmless Weapons by B.B. Gunn

595. Surrounded in Protection by Barry Cade

596. Walking with Cowboys by Beau Legged

597. Defensive Blockades by Bill Jerome Wall

598. Cowboys and Indians by Bowen Arrow

599. The Last Battle by R. Mageddon

600. Miniature Victories by Anthon Hill

MILITARY 2

601. Bullet Proof Vests Work by Pah Ding

602. Friend or Foe by Hugo Stair

603. The Wonders of Body Armour by Kev Larr

604. Massive Victory by M. Fatic

605. Military Disasters by Major Lee Badd

606. Hitting the Target by Mark Smann

607. Weapons of Mass Destruction by Miss Isle

608. Rotten Shot by Mr. Completely

609. Completely Surrounded by N. Gulfed

610. Great to be a Buccaneer by Phil E. Buster

MILITARY 3

611. Think you can Beat us? by Ewen Hugh Zarmee

612. Throwing Weapons by Tommy Hawk

613. Scandinavian Warriors by Vi King

614. Getting Ready for Action by Sue Tupp

615. Rebounding Bullets by Rick O'Shea

616. The Courageous Few by Val E. Ant

617. Thoroughly Defeated by Van Quish

618. We Won by Victor Ree

619. Meeting the Military by Sal Ute

620. Mowing them Down by Tommy Gunn

MOTIVATIONAL

621. Gain Control by B. A. Sertive

622. Leading the Way by Guy Ding

623. Optimism is Easy by Bea Positive

624. Everything Worked out Well by Bob Suruncle

625. Really Going For It by Buster Gutt

626. No Fear of Failure by Carrie Aunree-Gardless

627. From the Brink by Claude Bacc

628. Not Hard by E. Zee

629. Better than Brilliant by Fan Tastic

630. Pessimism is Easy by B. Negative

1001 Batty Books

MOTIVATIONAL 2

631. Better Than Great by Juan Der Full

632. It Will Happen by Mark Miwords

633. Going Ahead no Matter What by Raynor Schein

634. Find your Inner Self by Moe Joe

635. Moving Forward by Moe Mentum

636. I Can Get you Started by Moe T. Vator

637. Unhappy Person by Mona Lott

638. Striving Hard by N. Deverring

639. Don't Give Up by Percy Veer

640. A Successful Person by Moe Gull

MOTIVATIONAL 3

641. I'll Get you There by Sal Vation

642. Get it Together by Shay Pupp

643. Great News by Sue Perr

644. That's Wonderful by Terry Fick

645. Setting the Level by Stan Dard

646. Going Ahead by Will Doo

647. Putting Up With it All by N. Dure

648. Strength of Mind by Will Power

649. Get Real by Ria Lystic

650. I Give Up by U. Winn

MUSIC

651. Saving the Choir by Justin Tune

652. Below the Soprano by Al Toe

653. Man's Singing Voice by Barry Tone

654. Latin Music by Cass Tenets

655. Singing you a Love Song by Sarah Nade

656. The End of the Show by Kurt Anfalls

657. James Bond Theme by Liv N. Letdye

658. Deep Choir Sounds by Milo Voice

659. Symphony Sounds by Phil Armonic

660. In the Orchestra by Clara Nett

NATURE

661. A Deep Hole by A. Biss

662. Huge Items by E. Normous

663. Dead Flowers by M. T. Potts

664. Minerals that Glitter by Chris Tall

665. Return to the Wild by Freda Bird

666. Bush Fires by Flint Sparks

667. Showing off your Trees by Iva Forrest

668. Starting a Fire by Kindle Ling

669. Shelter from the Wind by Lee Ward

670. Volcanic Activity by E. Ruption

NATURE 2

671. Populating the Earth by P. Pull

672. Fires Don't Last by Peter Out

673. The Earth is Moving by Shay King

674. Rigid Poles by Stan Chun

675. Forest Truths by Theresa Greene

676. The Wild Frontier by Will de Ness

677. Dense Vegetation by Woody Forrest

678. Take Time to Smell the Flowers by Rose Bush

679. Autumn Noises by Russell Leaves

680. Keeping up your Tent by Guy Ropes

NIGHTTIME

681. Can't Sleep by Y. De Wake

682. Soft Steps by Ginger Leigh

683. Warm at Night by Ida Downe

684. Dripping all Night by Lee Kee Tapp

685. Rusty Bedsprings by I. P. Nightly

686. Insomnia by Liza Wake

687. Let There be Light by Wai So Dim

688. Too Much Noise by A. B. Quiet

689. Is Tonight On? by Willie Ornott

690. Peeping Toms by Pierre Vuzee Keehol

NOSES & SMELLS

691. The Great Unwashed by Ivan Oder

692. Bad Breath by Hal E. Toesis

693. Pollen Issues by Al R. Gees

694. Huge Noses by Ivor Biggun

695. Body Odor by Stin Ki Pu

696. He Smells by Willie Shower

697. No Deodorant by Willie Smell

698. Bubbles in the Spa by I. M. Windy

699. The Garlic Eater by I. Malone

700. Bubbles in the Bathtub by Ivor Windybottom

PAINFUL

701. Deadly Diseases by Anne Thrax

702. Looks Like Piles by Emma Roids

703. First Aid Now by Patch Meeup

704. Tetanus Causes by Rusty Nail

705. Dull Pain by A. King

706. More Accidents by Miss Takes and Miss Happs

707. Into Bondage by Ty Meup

708. High Pitched Noises by Wilma Glass-Brake

709. Still Crying? by Lee Nonmee

710. Stubbed My Foot by Toby Hurtting

PEOPLE

711. Answers the Door to Strangers by Hu Yu Arr

712. Paranoid Thoughts by R. U. Followin

713. Getting Desperate by Annie Wonwilldo

714. Good Manners by Bea Nice

715. Very Cool Reception by Cole der Zice

716. Tell me what you Saw by Dee Scribe

717. Meeting Famous People by Otto Graf

718. Very Smooth Gent by Deb O'Nare

719. Looking for Volunteers by N. E. Won

720. Nosy Neighbours by Annette Kirton

PEOPLE 2

721. Avoid the Crowds by Stan Dalone

722. All Rise by Stan Dupp

723. My Other Name by Sue D. Nimm

724. Welcome Everybody by Ree Seption

725. Looking in the Mirror by Van Ittie

726. Networks by Chris Cross

727. Meeting New People by How. R Yoo

728. Greeting Strangers by Hugh R. Yu

729. Opposites Attract by Maggie Nett

730. Impatient People by May Kumwait

POLITICAL

731. A Title of Nobility by Mark Wiss

732. Gain Votes by A. Pealing

733. Government Handouts by Benny Fitz

734. Out of your Depth by Noah Deer

735. Standing for President by E. Lection

736. How to be Knighted by Neil Down

737. Political Correctness by Noah Fence

738. Legal Matters by Sue Yu

739. Strongly State your Case by Ria Firm

740. Current Affairs by Daley News

PROBLEMS

741. Gambling Tales by Henrietta Hat

742. Two Equal Choices by Dai Lemmer

743. It's Not Real by Hal U. Sinations

744. Incorrect Theories by Sum Ting Wong

745. Not Proud of what I did by Ash Aimed

746. He's Coming for You by Bess U. Runn

747. Easily Broken by Britt Tull

748. Muck on the Wall by Hu Flung Dung

749. Puzzling Situations by Con Undrum

750. Gambling Tips by Winsom Cash

PROBLEMS 2

751. Set Back by Del Tablow

752. Hallucinations by Del U. Shun

753. No Ideas by Ed Scratcher

754. Helping Out by Linda Hand

755. Insurmountable Problem by Major Setback

756. Stranded in Town by Mr. Buss

757. Not Getting Anywhere by Noah Veil

758. Getting into Debt by Owen Moore

759. Quick Fixes by Pat Chupp

760. Can't Find a Way Out by A. Maize

PROBLEMS 3

761. Irish Failures by Troy Agin

762. Woman in Trouble by Warner Quick

763. It's Not Fair by Y. Mee

764. Terrible Karaoke by Yu Don Singh Well

765. It's Unavoidable by Sue Nora Later

766. Causing Trouble by Terry Rist

767. Complete Uncertainty by R. U. Shaw

768. Embarrassing Situations by Red Faced

769. Get Lost in the Woods by Wanda Off

770. Greenhouse Disasters by Chuck Stones

RELATIONSHIPS

771. Anyone Will Do by Des Pratt

772. My Doppleganger by Iva Dubble

773. Just Us! by Ewen Mee

774. Attracting Girls by Chick Magnet

775. This Way Please by Derek Shunn

776. In Between by Gaynor Strait

777. Missing you Already by Harry Bach

778. Solitary Confinement by I. Malone

779. Shy and Reserved by Tim Idd

780. He's in Love by Caeser Offen

RELATIONSHIPS 2

781. Not Restricted by Lee Way

782. Friends Again by Les B. Nice

783. Not as I Thought by Miss Judged

784. Giving Authority by N. Abe Ling

785. Deciding What you See by Phil Turing

786. We're all Family by R.U. McCousin

787. Capturing my Heart by Wynn Mee Ova

788. Holding Out Hope for Love by Yule Fynder

789. Getting Next to Others by Si Dillup

790. Listen Closely by I. Wispa

RELIGIOUS

791. How to Avoid Sin by A. Christian Upbringing

792. Closing Prayer by Bennie Diction

793. Religious Beliefs by Chris Tiann

794. It's Inevitable by Des Tinney

795. Burning in Hell by Lucy Furr

796. Where Monks Live by Moe Nastaries

797. Deep in Prayer by Neil Ling

798. Carrying Caskets by Paul Bearer

799. Religious Hostility by Percy Kution

800. End of the Line by Pearl E. Gates

SCARY STUFF

801. Hallucinations by Si Kosis

802. A Little Scared by Ann Ziety

803. I'm Really Worried by Anne Guish

804. Evil Spirits by Dee Mons

805. Look at That! by Ho Lee Cow

806. Unexplained Events by Mr. Ease

807. You Surprised Me by Omar Gosh

808. Horror Stories by R. U. Scared

809. A Trip to the Dentist by Terry Fied

810. This House is Haunted by Hugo First

SCIENCE

811. Computer Pictures by Ava Tarr

812. Computer Fixes by Dee Bugg

813. Introduction to Technology by P.C. Lerner

814. Wiring your Electrics by Alec Tricity

815. It's Huge! by Carl Ossel

816. Theories Proved Wrong by Dee Bunked

817. Hidden Meanings by E. Nigma

818. Just the Basic Parts by Ellie Mence

819. Where Did I Come From? by Gene Poole

820. Making Monsters by Frank N. Stein

SCIENCE 2

821. Leaders in the Tech Field by Mike Row Soft

822. Looking at Small Items by Moe Leck-Ular

823. Write in Code by N. Crypt

824. Early Warning Detection by Ray Darr

825. Which Comes First? by Orson Carte

826. It Might Work by Thea Retically

827. See Everything by X. Ray Specks

828. It's not Practical by Theo Ree

829. Just About Everywhere by U. Bickwittus

830. No TV Signal by Ray Deo

SEA & THE BEACH

831. Deep in the Ship by Belle O. Decks

832. Floatation Devices by Bob Inaround

833. It's Nice to Be by C. Side

834. Beautiful Views by Cliff Topp

835. Avoid Waves in Wales by Dai Vunder

836. Taking the Plunge by Di Ving

837. Boarding Ships by M. Bark

838. Releasing the Sea Giants by Freda Wales

839. Effective Sun Lotion by Justin Casey Burns

840. Cliff Tragedy by Eileen Dover

SEA & THE BEACH 2

841. Collision at Sea by Mandy Lifeboat

842. Nude Sunbathing by Oliver Klozoff

843. Seaside Activities by Rhoda Donkey

844. Sunbathing Opportunity by Sandy Beach

845. Huge Waves by Sue Narmie

846. Stop Drowning by Xavier Breath

847. Sitting on the Beach by Sandy Cheeks

848. Difficult Walk to the Water by Shelley Beech

849. Life on the Docks by Steve Adore

850. Battling Whales by Moe B. Dick

SHOPPING

851. Flashy Jewelry by Jules Sparkles

852. Ladies Accessories by Fay Keerings

853. Cheap Clothing by Polly Ester

854. Supermarket Shopping by Carrie R. Bag

855. Credit Card is Full by Max Stout

856. Sold Out! by M. T. Shelves

857. Slashing Prices by Mark Down

858. Selling your Goods by Mark Ette

859. A Day Shopping by Spencer Munny

860. Shopping in the Sales by Hans Fulle

SPACE

861. Outer Space Adventures by Sy Fi

862. Visitors from Outer Space by A. Lee Anne

863. Floating in Space by Andy Gravity

864. Twin Stars by Gemma Nye

865. Astrology Secrets by Horace Cope

866. Space Warriors by Jed Dye

867. Unbelievable Sci-Fi by May Trix

868. Star Trek Travel by N. R. Jize

869. Alien Weapons by Ray Gunn

870. Robots by Anne Droid

SPORTS & GAMES

871. Breaking Soccer Rules by Anne Ball

872. Olympic Games by Arthur Letics

873. Competition Winner by Bea First

874. We Lost by Bea Ten

875. Effective Basketball by Duncan Baskets

876. Can't Be Beaten by Bess Tattit

877. Running all Day Long by Betty Akes

878. Beginners Guide to Ice Skating by Betty Falls

879. Another Round of Poker by Dee L. Meehan

880. Pleasures on the Lake by Beau Ting

SPORTS & GAMES 2

881. All Croatian Tennis Players have Supernatural Powers by Goran Evaneesawitch

882. Gymnastics by Horace Zontalbars

883. I missed the Race by Hugh Wun

884. Fishing Accidents by I. B. Hooked

885. Russian Wrestling by Ivor Torabolokov

886. Safety in Sports by Jock Strap

887. Narrow Victories by Juan Nill

888. Slow Runner by Lars Twon Home

889. Last One Picked by Leigh Sliked

890. Kung Foo Moves by Marsha Larts

SPORTS & GAMES 3

891. Swinging Arms by Luke Out

892. Chasing Big Game Fish by Marlon Fisher

893. Megaphone Uses by Lowden Clear

894. Keeping Old Trophies by Moe Mentoes

895. Terrible Striker by Mr. Goal

896. Winning Streaks by Ona Role

897. Tennis Racquet Repairs by Rees Strung

898. Fairground Raffles by Tom Bola

899. Leading in Euro Sports by Francis Winning

900. A Round of Golf by T. Off

THAT'S A MESS

901. Waste Water by Sue Ridgepipe

902. It's Gonna Blow by Dai Namite

903. Baking with Kids by May Kinnemess

904. Mopping Spilt Drinks by Andy Towel

905. Dropped Rubbish Bins by Juan Hellofamess

906. Wet Carpets by Rufus Lee King

907. Smashed Plate Glass by Eva Brick

908. Messy Box Fillers by Polly Styrene

909. Rescued Junk by Sal Vige

910. Going to Deface it by Van da Lize

TIME

911. End of the Year by Dee Cemburr

912. Coming After Ten by E. Leven

913. Nearly Late by Justin Thyme

914. Always Waiting by Eva Ready

915. Most of the Time by General Lee Speaking

916. End of a Long Week by Gladys Friday

917. A Terrible Year by Helen Back

918. Start of the New Year by Jan U. Weery

919. Are you Done? by Jeff Inishyet

920. Remember Forever by Elle Lee Phant

TIME 2

921. I'm Nearly Ready by Lee Ving Soon

922. Procrastination Tips by May B. Tomorrow

923. I'm Not Ready by Wai Yu Kum Nao

924. About to Do it by Moe Mentarily

925. Just Yesterday by Reece Sent

926. It's Going to Happen by Sir Tenn

927. Life is Too Short by Y.B. Serious

928. Caring for the Future by Prue Dent

929. Female De Ja Vu by Zena Beffore

930. Seconds of Time by Mo Mence

TRAVEL

931. Motorways Blocked by Stan Dingstill

932. Negative Arabs by Sheikh Yahead

933. Transportable by Moe Bile

934. Get Moving by Sheikh Alegg

935. Sand on your Clothes by Sheikh Itoff

936. Life on a Submarine by Perry Scope

937. Hard Driving Surface by Ash Fault

938. Launch your Yacht by Beau Tramp

939. I'm Off Now by C. U. Later

940. Bike Repairs by Ben Tweel

TRAVEL 2

941. Out in the Country by Dusty Rhodes

942. Moving Between Floors by Ella Vader

943. A Little Piece of Home Soil by Em Bassy

944. Courageous Germans by Herr Rhoics

945. Proud Drivers by Iona Ford

946. Taking Lots of People by Ionna Buss

947. Do you want a Lift? by Ionna Carr

948. Taking People Across the Water by Ionna Ferri

949. Taking Even More People by Ionna Train

950. Backpacking Holiday by Lester Carry

TRAVEL 3

951. Mexican Love by Judy Won

952. Here We Go! by Liv Toff

953. Coming Out by M. Urge

954. Indian Concierge Tasks by Mahatma Cote

955. Long Walk Home by Miss D. Buss

956. Walking the Long Route by Sarah Nutherway

957. See the World by X. Plorer

958. Once Around the Block by Sir Kitt

959. Ready to Go by Stan Bye

960. Mobile Homes by Winnie Bago

WEATHER

961. We are Flooding! by Mandy Pumps

962. Fine Weather in India by Abu Tiffleday

963. Frozen Water by I. Sickle

964. Loose in the Wind by Ty Down

965. Spring Rains by April Showers

966. The Storm is Coming by Gail Force

967. Miserable Weather by Cole Danwett

968. Cold Winter Morning by Dewey Grass

969. It's All Gone Dark by E. Clips

970. Winter on the Hill by Bob Sled

WEATHER 2

971. Choppy Seas by Gale Forswins

972. Its Cold Out There by I. Swarning

973. Strange Weather by L. Nino

974. Gales and Storms by Wynne D. Wether

975. Thick Fog by P. Soop

976. Another Wet Afternoon by Ray Ning

977. Lovely Weather by Summer Sear

978. Downpour by Wayne Dwops

979. It's Cold Outside by Wynn Turr

980. It's so Hot by Mel Ting

WINNERS & LOSERS

981. Good Vibrations by Ree Verb

982. The Absolute Best by Sue Peerior

983. Caught off Guard by Sir Prize

984. Poor Skills by Terri Bull

985. Plain and Boring by Vann Illa

986. Keep Things Going by Warren Tee

987. Over and Above by X. Traa

988. Won't be Last by Wynn Attlecosts

989. On the Way Out by X. Itt

990. Always a Loser by Wyn Nuffin

AND FINALLY...

991. Stop Messing Around by Gita Life

992. You're Doing Fine Now by Howard Yuno

993. Adding Detail by L. Aborate

994. I Want You by Kum Hia Now

995. Unrequired by Sue Purrfluous

996. All the Names on the List by Reggie Stir

997. Colour Sketches by Drew A. Peacock

998. Caged Birds by Bud Gee

999. Fantasy Animals by U. Nick Horn

1000.   Not Bothered by Hugh Cares

AND FINALLY FINALLY...

1001.   Lost German Boy by Yvonne Der Zoff

ABOUT THE AUTHORS

Derek and Craig have been business partners since 2003 and enjoy a good laugh. Their online training company, www.learningplanet.me is all about providing bite sized chunks of learning normally through video with a tinge of humour to help the message be memorable. Both originally from England, they have settled in New Zealand with their respective families and enjoy the wonderful climate, laid back lifestyle and the flexibility to have a good laugh while working for a living!

1001 Batty Books has been a number of years in the making. In 2015, the duo finally made it a priority and scoured the world for great 'pun' names to add to the book with some of the best coming from moments of pure inspiration. The authors hope you enjoy reading them as much as they enjoyed compiling them!

25550695R00118

Printed in Great Britain
by Amazon